*REAL*ationships

*REAL*ationships: The Real Truth About Dating, Marriage, and Divorce

*REAL*ationships:
The Real Truth About Dating, Marriage, and Divorce

EARNEST FITZHUGH, II

*REAL*ationships: The Real Truth About Dating, Marriage, and Divorce

Earnest Fitzhugh, II, has been preaching since the age of seventeen and has been in pastoral ministry since 2009. He was licensed at age nineteen, and ordained as an elder by the late Bishop LeRoy Robert Anderson a year later. He served as an associate elder of Higher Ground Church of God in Christ in Phoenix, AZ, where his father is pastor. He now pastors Redemption Life Center in Phoenix, AZ. He and his wife, "Rey," proudly parent four children and continue to aspire to do God's work and be an example for those around them.

For more information about the author, visit
www.realationshipsbook.com.

Copyright © 2019 by Earnest Fitzhugh, II.

All rights reserved.

No part of this publication may be reproduced or distributed in any form or by any means, or stored in a database or retrieval system, without the prior written permission of the publisher. Email requests for permission to ministeringpurpose@gmail.com.

PurposeHouse Publishing
Columbia, Maryland
Visit our website at http://publishing.purposehouse.net.

Printed in the United States of America.

ISBN: 978-0-9963647-4-4

Unless otherwise indicated, all scriptural quotations are from the King James Version of the Bible, which is in the public domain.

Scripture from New King James Version (NKJV), Copyright © 1982 by Thomas Nelson, Inc., All rights reserved.

Scripture from the Wycliffe Bible (WYC), copyright © 2001 by Terence P. Noble.

DEDICATION

This book is dedicated to my wife, "Rey." You were the tool God used to bring me hope and restore my faith in relationships at all levels. This book is for you and because of you.

CONTENTS

Dedication	*vii*
Acknowledgements	*xi*

PART I: UNDERSTAND GOD'S PURPOSE, PROCESS, AND DESIGN FOR RELATIONSHIPs

Introduction	*3*
Chapter 1: Purpose Drives Preparation	9
Chapter 2: Company or Companionship?	15
Chapter 3: Man was Formed: Woman was Fashioned	21
Chapter 4: Does God Choose Your Spouse?	27

PART II: CONSIDERATIONS WHEN CHOOSING: WHAT I WISH I HAD KNOWN

Chapter 5: Discovery Versus Pursuit	37
Chapter 6: False Advertisement	41
Chapter 7: Understanding Influences	49

PART III: MAKE SURE YOU'RE HEALED

Chapter 8: Cheating and Temptation	61
Chapter 9: Forgiveness	69

PART IV: PREPARE YOUR MARRIAGE FOR SUCCESS

Chapter 10: No Deal Breakers	77
Chapter 11: Boundaries	83
Chapter 12: Reciprocation	91

ACKNOWLEDGMENTS

To My Parents: I've watched you model marriage successfully my entire life. Thank you for showing me that it works, when you do it right.

To My Children: Thank you for being resilient throughout every one of my relationship transitions. The wisdom I've gained came with a great cost, and sometimes you all paid the price. Thank you for never loving me less.

To my wife: Thank you for being patient with my countless hours on the computer, writing, designing and analyzing. You've never complained and even have pushed me to be a better man that I thought possible. Thank you for loving an imperfect "me," so perfectly.

To my church family: You've stuck through difficult seasons and kept me in prayer. You lifted me up when my head was down. And I'll be eternally grateful.

To my friends: My friends circle shrunk drastically, but the value of it skyrocketed. I don't use the term "friend" loosely anymore and I thank you for being one. You know who you are.

And finally, to my past: Thank you for the good moments and the bad. The ups and the downs. The people in it and people now out of it. You've been the driving force for this book and the basis for my desire to help others. I thank God for you and all that are in it.

PART I:
UNDERSTAND GOD'S PURPOSE, PROCESS, AND DESIGN FOR RELATIONSHIPS

INTRODUCTION

At seventeen, I started preaching. I got married at nineteen, and it lasted four years. Six weeks later, I married my second wife.

I'm not writing this book because I've gotten everything right. Through experience, I learned that there is a religious side of the Church that doesn't always facilitate real answers to real-life issues. Telling someone, "It's better to marry than to burn," or "never get a divorce," doesn't always address the practical issues confronting their marriage. There are real-life scenarios that the church doesn't always address.

For example, consider the events leading up to my first divorce at age twenty-three. I met with my bishop, and his wife told me I would never be a pastor, and I would never have a church if I left my wife. Before that meeting, my first wife and I had been going to marital counseling with them. During the counseling, my bishop told me things like, "You don't want another man to raise your children." There was a lot of "You don't want this… and you don't want that." But one day he pulled me to the side and said, "Son, obviously you know something that I don't know. I would never tell a man to stay with a woman he does not want. So whatever it is that you know that I don't know, you make that decision and be smart about it."

So, I opted for divorce, and approximately a year later, she revealed that she was a lesbian and had always had an attraction to women. She and I had significant problems after each child. I knew there were issues, but I kept trying to push through because my family raised me never to divorce. We each had issues that doomed that relationship to failure from the beginning. And had I looked for the warning signs or known what to look for, it would have been a different scenario. That was the only marriage in which I was the one who initiated divorce.

In life, people have to navigate challenging, complex situations. People have real issues and practical questions like, how do you handle infidelity? How do you deal with coparenting a child from your spouse's previous relationship? Who takes precedence in a blended family, the child who's always been there or the new step-parent? What is "Christian Dating?" There's nothing in the Scripture about Christian dating or God telling someone who their spouse is except Hosea and Gomer. Does God pick your spouse?

People often say that, but is there any Scripture to support that assertion? How is that we accept things as good marital advice when there's no clarity or biblical basis behind some things we say? We make a lot of assumptions and give a lot of opinions, but they don't align with Scripture.

My parents raised me to never divorce—never. I had heard that in the Church throughout my life, and my parents have a thirty-seven-year marriage. But having suffered through divorce multiple times, I thank God that I discovered some things in Scripture that can help couples overcome some pitfalls I endured. By the grace of God, the man that I am now is 100 times better than who I was at nineteen. I wrote this book because I want to help people overcome challenges I did not have the wisdom to overcome.

Through experience and the word of God, in this book, I address questions that others may shy away from or not even know how to address. This book will benefit anyone who wants to know how to build boundaries to protect their marriage, or who desires a successful relationship done God's way—whether already married, dating, or desiring to be in a relationship.

The Second Marriage

Six weeks after my first divorce, I married my second wife. Three months into my second marriage, I discovered my first (and then ex-wife) had a third child that I did not know about, my youngest son. She never told me she was pregnant. I knew she had been unfaithful during our marriage, and I assume she didn't tell me she was pregnant because she wasn't sure if the child was mine. I found out about my son (from the first wife) by seeing him with his brother and sister one day at daycare; finding out that way put a strain on my second marriage.

I knew my first wife had been unfaithful with a married man. She had quit her job, and instead of going to work, she was spending time with this man. I found out about it because her job called and asked if she would return her work materials. A day later, the man's wife called my house. She and I put things together, and we knew our spouses had been cheating together.

My second wife slept with her ex during the first week of our relationship. But I still wanted to push through that because I didn't want to go through another failed relationship. Even after the infraction, there were no boundaries—she still wanted to be close friends with her ex. He was always around, and that became a sore spot in the relationship, so it didn't last long. I came home from work the day after Thanksgiving to find her and her brothers loading up a truck. She said it was over. Perhaps because of the trust issues my ex-wife's pregnancy created, or because of her ex, she opted for divorce. Ironically, this marriage also lasted only four years.

The Third Marriage

I thought the third marriage would be the one that would make it. My third wife grew up in the Church and had never married. However, she had a working relationship with her child's dad. I met him, and he seemed to be an okay guy. But I always thought they were too close. I already had insecurities from my previous spouses being too close to their exes. She defended that under the premise that "We're just coparenting," and coparents should be able to friends. How do you fight that? I tried to be understanding and respectful of that.

Four to six months into the relationship, I glanced at a text and found out that their communication was sexual. I saw text messages where they were flirting, and her child's father was cracking jokes like, "You may still have my last name one day." Keep in mind; they had never married. I found out she had wanted to marry him, but he would never commit to her even though they had a child together. When I saw the texts, I assumed that they had probably been cheating, so she and I got into an argument about that. Afterward, I stepped outside of the relationship. I started seeing someone else. By that time, I had started the church.

Four months later, I called it off with the other woman I was seeing. We were both married, but she wanted me to leave my wife for her; I knew that would be wrong. She told her husband about it and thought I would have to tell my wife. In her mind, that would end my marriage.

My issue was boundaries. She and I had been friends for years. I was never the guy that women wanted to date growing up. So I became very comfortable being their best "guy" friend. My wife and I attended her wedding, and she and her husband had attended ours. She worked close to my job, and we were cool, so one day, she called me and mentioned that she needed money for lunch. So I went over. She was explaining some of her frustrations to me, and she kissed me, and that was it—the pedal had hit the medal. Again, my issue was boundaries. We were both married, and I could have put more distance in the relationship. When I ended it, she told her husband. I also told my third wife.

On a Sunday morning, I told my third wife that I had gotten involved with someone else. Someone who had been my friend for years, and with whom I had never expected to get into a romantic situation. Honestly, if the woman had not told her husband, I don't think I would have told my third wife. I knew she would assume it was in response to what I had found out about her and her communication with her child's father. I knew it would be bad from there. We went to a trusted pastor for counseling, the same counselor that did our premarital counseling. She said she forgave me and wanted to move forward, but I don't think we ever recovered.

As time passed, I noticed her relationship with her child's father grew even closer; it was as if the connection was stronger than ever. I watched her cry when she found out he was having a baby with another woman. As she heard the news from him on the phone, she sobbed and asked, "How come you didn't tell me you were having a baby with someone else?" When I asked her why it bothered her so much, in a moment of vulnerability, she admitted, *"Because I feel that someone else is taking my place."* Those words doomed us. I knew the relationship would end. Because of my offense, the sin of seeing someone else, our relationship became an unbalanced relationship. Sin diminishes our countenance before God and our spouse, and diminishes our dominion.

The moment Adam sinned, his spouse became the enemy. When God addressed the sin with him, he blamed his wife. We have to understand the impact of sin on our relationships. It impacts our spouse's loyalty and the way they view us. And even though they forgive, it may never change the diminished countenance that they see on us. You can rebuild and forgive, but something will always be different. We lose Eden when we allow sin to enter our marriage. Even though she said she wanted to move forward, after three years of trying and struggling, she ultimately opted for divorce.

I am transparently sharing my story so that, through this book, others can gain wisdom I had to get through painful experiences. But from the pain, I've gained a revelation that can prevent others from making the mistakes I made. The things I'm about to share will make a difference and bring victory in areas that confront marriages every day. I can speak about coparenting and boundaries from experience.

And from that same experience, I will show you that:

- The biblical way is the only way that's guaranteed to safeguard a relationship (the only guaranteed way).
- Being honest with yourself is the premise or basis for having a healthy relationship.
- Anybody can learn to have a healthy relationship.

Thank you for reading this book. I pray your relationship, whether current or future, gains strength and power through what you read.

1 PURPOSE DRIVES PREPARATION

I stood up. "When I get old, when I become a man, I'm going to be a preacher, I'm going to be a lawyer, and I'm going to be married with two kids," I said. It was Career Day. I was wearing a little suit with a tie, and I had a briefcase and a play wedding ring on my finger.

I was seven years old and in Ms. Jones' second-grade class. That day, we had to come to school dressed up as what we imagined ourselves being when we grew up. Even at seven, the three things that were most important to me were being a preacher, a lawyer, and married with kids.

I always intended to be married. I always envisioned that I would marry and have kids. Ultimately, I became a preacher, and I joined the legal field. I had been dreaming of marriage since age seven, so obviously, that was also very important to me. So at the early age of nineteen, I considered marriage important—a necessity. The challenge was, aside from having children (having a family), I never knew the purpose of marriage. At nineteen, I didn't understand God's design for marriage.

I couldn't answer questions like, what was marriage supposed to emulate? What was marriage supposed to be? How was it supposed to impact the rest of the world? I didn't understand the purpose. I just knew that I wanted to be married. I knew I wanted to have kids.

And when you don't understand the purpose of a thing, you don't prepare for it adequately.

When God created Adam, he did a few things before introducing him to the concept of marriage because God understood the purpose for which he created Adam and Eve. God knew the purpose for which he would unite them in marriage.

There are many believers and unbelievers alike who do not understand God's purpose for marriage. Yes, the Scripture says, "it's better to marry than to burn," but after sex, then what? Is that the only purpose of marriage? Surely, it's not. And when you understand that, you prepare differently. When you understand the purpose, there's a higher level of preparation.

God demonstrates this in Genesis chapters one and two. He prepares Adam before ever introducing him to the concept of marriage. He sets some things in place for Adam.

First, Adam had a place to live. God gives Adam a place to live; then, he gives Adam a purpose. He puts him in the Garden of Eden and tells him to till the ground. That was Adam's job—tilling the Garden. Before a man ever meets a woman that he can be a husband to, God must first place him. He needs to have a job and have dominion over his animals and wild things. That's the next thing God gave Adam—dominion over the animals.

Placed

> And the Lord God planted a garden eastward in Eden; and there he put the man whom he had formed. [9] And out of the ground made the Lord God to grow every tree that is pleasant to the sight, and good for food; the tree of life also in the midst of the garden, and the tree of knowledge of good and evil. (Genesis 2:8-9 KJV)

Before God presented Eve to Adam, God placed Adam. God situated him, planted him in a place that could sustain his basic needs for shelter and food. He had a stable living environment, a consistent place to lay his head at night. His life was not unstable. His atmosphere was stable enough for someone else to cohabit.

God gave Adam a job.

And the Lord God took the man, and put him into the Garden of Eden to dress it and to keep it. (Genesis 2:15 KJV)

Before Adam met Eve, he had a job. He was the gardener of the Garden of Eden. God gives him this assignment before he ever knows Eve because without an assignment or job for Adam, there was nothing in Adam's life that required Eve's help. She could not have been a helpmate without anything in his life that needed her help.

Dominion Over the Wild Things

> And out of the ground the Lord God formed every beast of the field, and every fowl of the air; and brought them unto Adam to see what he would call them: and whatsoever Adam called every living creature, that was the name thereof. [20] And Adam gave names to all cattle, and to the fowl of the air, and to every beast of the field; but for Adam there was not found an help meet for him. (Genesis 2:19-20 KJV)

He gave Adam dominion over the fowls and beasts and tells Adam whatever you call these animals; that's what their names will be. He gave Adam creative ability—ability to produce. Not only did Adam have a job and an assignment, but Adam also had control over the animals.

God did not present Eve until Adam named the animals.

Dominion over the animals preceded the presentation of his wife. Before he takes a wife, every man needs to have control over areas of his life that have gone wild. He needs to control the areas that still need subjection. If you don't have control over the areas that have gone wild, areas of struggle, you are not ready for marriage. Some of these areas might include issues with:

- Flesh: Struggles in your flesh may have gone wild. The fruit of the Spirit includes self-control. Some men believe that marriage is a cure for problems with lust and sexual immorality. If you don't tame these wild animals before you marry, they will cause damage and magnify themselves after you marry. Marriage is not a cure for lust or any other issue of the flesh. Tame your wild animals.
- Boundaries: You may lack appropriate boundaries with the opposite sex or with family members.
- Provision: Your finances may be wild.
- Living Condition: Have you been placed? Do you have a stable living environment?

Every man needs to have control over his animals before he ever tries to get married. Dominion over the animals preceded the presentation of a wife. That's the order in which God addresses things in Genesis.

Identity

Adam had a name—he had an identity. If you don't know who you are, or you struggle with your identity as a son of God, you're not ready for marriage.

Relationship with God

Adam had a relationship with God. He walked with God in the cool of the day in the Garden, and conversed with God. How can a husband hear God for his family, if he can't hear God for himself? How can he have a direction for his family or wife, if he doesn't have a direction for himself? There needs to be a daily walk with God. There should be consistency in his spiritual life, or else he's not ready to be a husband.

Because God understands the purpose for which he instituted marriage, he also models for us the necessary preparation. Being placed, having a job, controlling your animals, knowing your identity, and having a relationship with God are all prerequisites for marriage. These things need to be in place before even considering marriage. God made sure all these things were in place before he presented Eve to Adam, and he also wants them in place in your life before you consider marriage.

> *"By failing to prepare, you are preparing to fail."–Benjamin Franklin*

So commit to your time of preparation. Don't be in a rush. Like me, you may have dreamed of marriage since you were a child. But add preparation to your dream, so it doesn't become a nightmare.

It may not be your season for marriage. You may not be ready for true companionship. Depending on what season you're in, your life may only contain company and not companionship, which we discuss in the next chapter.

2 COMPANY OR COMPANIONSHIP?

I needed a woman to need me. But I wasn't looking for companionship. Instead, people who needed a "knight in shining armor," had daddy issues, or wanted what came with me, but didn't actually want me, drew my attention. Those people and I both wanted the same thing—the company. We didn't want to be lonely, but we weren't ready to commit to companionship.

God said, "It is not good that man should be alone." (Genesis 2:19 KJV) He announces that he will make the man a helper comparable to him. But in the meantime, the next thing God did was create animals.

When God addresses the fact that Adam was lonely, he created *company* before *companionship*. God creates animals before he presents Eve. To determine the purpose of a relationship, decide whether the relationship is for company, i.e., friendship, or for companionship, i.e., marriage. He created company for Adam before he created Eve for companionship. There's a difference.

He created the animals first. Then, he let Adam name them. "Out of the ground the Lord God formed every beast of the field and every bird of the air, and brought them to Adam to see what he would call them. And whatever Adam called each living creature, that was its name." (Genesis 2:19 NJKV)

The animals spent time with Adam. We know the animals could talk because the serpent could speak (Genesis 3:1-4). Also, we know animals could speak at some point. In the case of Balaam and Balak, the Scripture says that God opened the mouth of the donkey, which indicates that at some point, the donkey's mouth was shut.

"Then the Lord opened the mouth of the donkey, and she said to Balaam, "What have I done to you, that you have struck me these three times?" (Numbers 22:28 NKJV)

So now, Adam had company, but even then, that wasn't good enough. After God creates the animals, he says there is still not a helper suitable for Adam. Company can be there to keep you from being lonely. But companionship is a help that is meet, or suitable for you, and intended to walk with you at the highest levels of emotional, spiritual, and physical intimacy for the rest of your life.

To identify whether a person is company or companionship, take a step back and realize what you need and what the other person can offer. Often in my relationships, I realized they did not want me as a person—they wanted attention; they were lonely. They just wanted the company.

And you need not involve yourself with someone romantically to avoid loneliness or have company. Before you attach yourself to someone, releasing all kinds of romantic emotions and affections prematurely, ask yourself, "Is this because I'm lonely and need someone to hang out with, or is this suited for true companionship?" Also, please ask yourself, "Is this someone I want for the long haul, or I am with them because I don't want to be lonely now?"

Many people in relationships, or in "situation-ships," engage in romantic involvement with someone not because they want them, or want to spend the rest of their life with them, but because they want their attention. Some people just want company. They feel validated by having company and not being alone.

This is where so-called "Christian dating" can go utterly wrong. There is a tendency to be romantic when what you need is company. Can't we be brothers and sisters in Christ without romantic feelings entering? 1 Timothy 5:1-2 says, "Treat younger men as brothers, older women as mothers, and younger women as sisters, with absolute purity." (New International Version) Scripture doesn't even say anything about dating. It speaks about espousal, but not dating.

What is it about dating in the church that would differ from having a friendship? If we're not supposed to be physical, if it's not supposed to be sexual, then why can't you be a friend without the constant discussion about marriage? What will be different? How would we define Christian friends versus Christians who are dating? Is it who pays for the dinner bill? Is it that we hold hands, or we don't hold hands? Some Christians believe you don't even kiss before you get married. So how do we define it?

If the relationship is not sexual, then what's the problem with being friends? Is it because we need somebody to pay for our dinner? Is it because we need somebody to talk about family aspirations? But that could come up organically at the appropriate time if we discover that someone is aligned with our purpose.

It took me a long time to realize that sometimes I just wanted someone there, or sometimes, somebody just wanted me there for the moment but not for the future—not for the long haul. And it's essential to identify these things early to avoid having your feelings hurt later.

I'd find myself in relationships where people would only call me when they wanted something. They would call when they wanted to hang out, needed a hand, or had a bill they needed me to pay. However, I wouldn't hear from them anymore after that. They would talk to me consistently until we hung out, or they asked for something. But once they got what they wanted, whether it was financial, emotional, or physical, they would go silent—they would "ghost me." They wouldn't call. And it took me a long time to realize that I had more value than just being used for what I had, but my value was in who I was.

Many people find themselves entangled because they can't recognize the difference between company and companionship. Not everyone who keeps you from being lonely is suitable to be your spouse. Learn how to keep things on a friendship level when it's just company. Don't cross lines that require a level of commitment you never intended or wanted.

Don't cross the companionship line until you know who you are. Remember, God gave Adam identity before he presented Eve.

We have to know who we are first before we can assess what we want in a person. For example, you can't want a traditional man if you're not a traditional woman. How can two walk together unless they agree? You can't want an alpha male if you're an alpha female—it will not work. You will bump heads. So you have to know who you are, what you want, and what you desire before you can join with anybody. And I believe that many people don't know who they are and that's why they fail horribly in relationships because they haven't taken the time to know who they are.

Many people talk about wanting a Boaz, but they are far from being a Ruth.

You have to know who you are to assess who's a good fit for you effectively. God will give you a choice, and to make a good choice, be honest with yourself. There's no other way to know who will be a good companion for you.

Companionship has a higher purpose and requires a greater commitment.

"And the Lord God said, "It is not good that man should be alone; I will make him a helper comparable to him." (Genesis 2:18 NKJV)

God designed companionship to bring help, not hindrances. That's why the preparation and prerequisites discussed in Chapter One are so important. It's difficult to bring someone in to help mess. And, people who are company don't always have what it takes to be suitable helpers.

That applies to both men and women. Hanging out with someone differs from helping them build a life, a future. To help me, you must be comparable to me spiritually, emotionally, mentally, and financially.

A person can be great to hang out with and be around. They can be the life of the party and humorous. Or they could be a great listener and very empathetic; you could enjoy hanging out with them. Still, that doesn't guarantee they have what it takes to help you build a future—whether in the marketplace, ministry, or both. Remember, the Bible specified, "a helper suitable." Everyone who can help isn't always suitable for you.

A helper comparable to me is someone who builds me, helps to expand and enlarge my territory, multiplies me, and can help take dominion. So don't get company twisted with companionship.

The animals were company, but they were not enough for companionship. So God put Adam to sleep.

Sleep is a still state.

Before God presents Eve to Adam, he puts him in a still state. A man who does not know how to be still or who has not settled down is not ready for marriage. Are you still too busy? Do you still have too much going on?

If you see a man who always wants to be here, there, and everywhere, he's not ready for marriage. If there's still no structure to his life or no settling in him, he's not ready to take on the responsibilities of caring and leading somebody else. He's not settled.

If he's still halting between two opinions—he's non-committal and not embracing preparation for the future—he's not settled. A double-minded man is unstable in all his ways. He needs to be settled in his mind, finances, lifestyle, character, demeanor, and prayer/devotional life. Then and only then will he be ready for a spouse because the Scripture says God puts Adam to sleep, takes a bone from Adam, and creates a woman.

God formed the man from dust, but he fashioned the woman from a bone.

3 MAN WAS FORMED: WOMAN WAS FASHIONED

As we were driving home, I had asked my wife, "What do you want to eat?" and she replied, "Oh, I don't know, you pick."

I said, "Well, I want to make sure I know what you want to eat because I don't want to pick the wrong thing. So I just want to make sure I know. So just go ahead and tell me what you don't want, and I'll try to select from what you possibly do want."

So after about five or ten minutes, she said, "Well, I don't want Chinese. And I don't want Mexican. I don't want burgers because we just had that."

Okay, that was fine, so after a while of thinking, I was like, "You know, we'll do Italian, how about that? We'll do Italian."

"No, I don't want that," she replied.

I immediately got frustrated because I specifically asked her what did she did not want, so I could know what to pick.

As a result, I was silent on the way home, and she would say, "What's wrong?"

I would say, "Nothing."

She would keep asking, "What's wrong?" and I would say, "Nothing, don't worry about it. I'm okay."

And then, we get home, and now her attitude has changed. I ask her, "What's wrong?" And she says, "Well, nothing."

"Well, what is it? What's the problem?" I asked.

"Well, nothing," she said.

I became frustrated by the circumstances. I'm thinking to myself, well first, I was irritated. I've let it go, and now she's irritated.

So, finally, about twelve hours later, I'm like, "So what's wrong with you?"

"Well, you always shut down when I want to have a conversation about something. Yesterday, I asked you what's wrong, and you didn't say anything. So then that made me upset. And now, I don't want to talk at all," she explained.

At that moment, I realized how different men are versus women. The one conversation that irritated me, and I didn't want to have a discussion about what bothered me turned into, "You always shut down." She didn't isolate what was happening to that situation. Her assessment expanded across that situation and others. So now it turned into, "You always do this."

To me, it seemed extreme, but to her, it seemed valid. Then, I realized how men and women interpret things differently. It made me think about Adam and Eve, how God formed the man from dust, but he fashioned the woman.

Think about how men have a great ability to compartmentalize things. If something happens at eight o'clock this morning, we *can have an attitude maybe for an hour or two. After that, we will reset, and we'll be fine because we compartmentalize our feelings. It will not impact our whole day.*

However, many times for women, if something irritates her at that moment and it's not resolved in a fashion that's acceptable to her, that one occurrence can spread across the entire day. It can cause an impact on dinner or the next day because there's no resolution in her mind.

What men seem to be able to bypass, sometimes women hold to a higher regard or a higher level of importance. And until as individuals, we understand that God wired us differently, arguments and situations can blow out of proportion because we do not understand each other's needs.

Men are simpler in how they process. But for women, everything is connected. I would almost say a thread connects everything, and if any part of that thread is impacted, it impacts every other thing. So I've learned from that standpoint always to remember, I was made, but she was fashioned.

Anytime a designer fashions something, it's more complex than something that he formed. The Scripture says God put Adam to sleep; and then took a bone from Adam and created a woman. He formed the man from dust; he fashioned the woman from bone.

We often talk about how women can handle things that men cannot. I believe that's a very accurate statement. A man may be physically stronger sometimes. But with what's underneath the surface, when it comes to the bone, women seem to be stronger and more intricate. For example, a woman can handle childbirth, something men cannot handle. And they seem to handle emotional things that men cannot. God wired men and women differently.

Fashioned

In Genesis 2:7, the word *formed* means squeezed out and shaped like clay[1]. In Genesis 2:22, the word *fashioned* means built, erected, faceted like a house is designed and built[2]. Compare the work of a potter with the work of an architect. You will find that one is more complex, involves more tasks and materials than the other.

Man	Woman
Then the Lord **God formed man** of dust from the ground, and breathed into his nostrils the breath of life; and man became a living being. (Genesis 2:7 NASB)	The LORD **God fashioned into a woman** the rib which He had taken from the man, and brought her to the man. (Genesis 2:22 NASB)
Potter and clay	Architect and home

The Scripture says that God formed Adam but fashioned the woman. Fashioned means she's intricate. She's made peculiarly as a species. She's different, unique, and not the same as a man. She should be treated differently than a man, not from the standpoint of inequality, because we know they were both given dominion. In Genesis 1:26, God blessed both of them and told them both to take dominion. However, a woman,

---

[1] "Formed," Blue Letter Bible, accessed November 28, 2019, https://www.blueletterbible.org/lang/Lexicon/Lexicon.cfm?strongs=H3335&t=KJV.
[2] "Made," Blue Letter Bible, accessed November 28, 2019, https://www.blueletterbible.org/lang/Lexicon/Lexicon.cfm?strongs=H1129&t=KJV.

specifically a wife, should be treated differently from the standpoint of design. Her design is more intricate. She's high fashion.

Understanding these differences and complexities can help people navigate a relationship successfully. Take the conversation my wife and I had about what to eat. Men tend to be simpler. Women tend to be more in-depth. A man can take a sentence and mean what he says. A woman can take a sentence and turn it into an entire paragraph.

Use this information to form your communication and navigate conversations. She doesn't think the way you do, and you don't think the way she does. She will make connections you never put together. Understand that it's not an attack. That's the way she's wired.

Multipliers

God designed women to be multipliers by nature. God does not give the command to be fruitful and multiply until Eve arrives on the scene.

> So God created man in his own image, in the image of God created he him; male and female created he them. 28 And God blessed them, and God said unto them, Be fruitful, and multiply, and replenish the earth, and subdue it: and have dominion over the fish of the sea, and over the fowl of the air, and over every living thing that moveth upon the earth. (Genesis 1:27-28 KJV)

I believe women have an innate ability to multiply. I believe it's wired into their genetics not only spiritually but naturally. Think about it. A man gives a woman a seed, and she creates a baby. She takes a house, and she makes it a home. Women can multiply and do things that it seems most men cannot do.

They are God-given multi-taskers. They seem to handle and juggle so many things most men cannot. With most men, if you give them one assignment, by the time they get to the second one, they've forgotten what number one was. But women can handle fifteen different things and seem to do them all effectively. A man needs to focus on a single task. A man can't remember what you talked about last week. A woman can bring up something that happened two years ago with specificity.

She's a rib.

God made Eve from a rib because it's the rib's design to protect the most important organs in the body. The rib's design was literally to protect the heart. So a woman's created to be a rib and not a thorn. But when a woman is hurt, she becomes rough, jagged, and broken. She changes from a rib to a thorn and can tear down her man the way nobody else can. That is why a man will not be upset when another man talks about him. But when his woman talks about him, it tears him down in a way nobody else can.

God wired us differently, and if we don't understand these differences, it can lead to misunderstandings. Don't despise the differences. They are there to be a blessing to you. A companion needs to multiply and help take dominion. Know the difference between company and companion, and formed and fashion so that you can make the right choice.

4 DOES GOD CHOOSE YOUR SPOUSE?

I got married at nineteen. I always knew I would get married even before Ms. Jones' second-grade class. I always knew I would have kids. It was high on my priority list. At nineteen, I met someone who gave me attention and seemed to fit what I desired in a spouse.

Despite obvious signs that should have caused me to think twice about my decision, we got married. Despite some challenges, mostly, it was good for the first year. But right after the first year, we got pregnant with my son. And towards the birth of my son, we really began to have issues.

Later, when my daughter was born, we were separating, and that's challenging because, as Christians, we don't believe in divorce. We believe God doesn't like it, and God brings you together. So, we were still trying to work it out despite signs of infidelity and a lack of unity. We tried again a third time to make it work. It didn't work.

After we realized it didn't work, I filed for divorce. During that time, we lived in separate places. The divorce hearing was in October. I had met someone else right before our divorce hearing and started dating her; I started engaging in a relationship with her.

About thirty days after my divorce, I got married again. I didn't tell anyone, not even my parents, until after we had gotten married. That was the first sign that it probably wasn't the right thing to do. But I felt confident that we could work. We had gone to grade school together; everything progressed quickly. And because they teach you it's better to marry than to burn, I wanted to make sure I did my best in at least honoring God in that area, so we got married and combined families quickly.

Right after that, unbeknownst to me, my first wife (now ex-wife) had another baby. She didn't share that she was pregnant. And I have suspicions why she didn't share. Because of infidelity, she probably wasn't sure whether I was the father of the child. She had another baby after I'd already re-married. And that created difficulty in that second marriage. Anytime people would ask me about that second marriage, I would always say, "I chose her." I never blamed or gave God credit for bringing us together. Keep in mind; I was twenty-three years old. But I never gave God credit for it because deep down, I knew that it was my choice, not realizing that over time I'd gain a greater revelation about choice.

Unfortunately, the second marriage didn't last. She decided she wanted a divorce. There were trust issues for her and for me, and ultimately, we didn't work. She left, and I said, "God, I'm going to wait. I'm not going to rush." And it wasn't until after my divorce was final with her, that I met my third wife.

When I met my third wife, she was in the Church. She sang, her dad was a musician, and her family was in the Church. We met through church friends. We grew up in the same town. Everything seemed to make sense. I thought, this one must be

God. It had to be God. There's no reason it wouldn't have been God. Things were great, but in the first year, there were some concerns and issues regarding boundaries and infidelity.

All these issues came up in what I thought was the perfect relationship. I thought this was the person who God chose because obviously, I must have missed it with the first two marriages, right? God must have chosen her; he must have put us together. We put God's name on it and had a big, beautiful church wedding. Only to discover, there were some unresolved issues in former relationships that ended up being cancer to our relationship. We didn't make.

I mean, listen, everything about that relationship seemed as if "God put us together," but we didn't make it. So, I realized that everything about our relationship had to be about choice. If God makes no mistake, if we say it is God every time, then when was God wrong? If we say it's God every time and God does not believe in divorce, was it God the first time? The second time? The third time?

How do we in the church justify remarriage? And granted, some people don't believe in remarriage, and we'll leave that to them and their theology. But the Bible talks about means for divorce. There was divorce in Biblical times. The causes and reasons for it deal with the hardness of the heart.

But if it's God that picked it, and God knows the end from the beginning, which marriage was wrong?

I finally realized, there's a deeper revelation for the selection of a spouse, and that we've put much more responsibility on God than he takes credit for in the Scripture. Every believer has a responsibility in selecting a spouse.

Never do we find in the Genesis account where God called Eve Adam's spouse. God never called Eve, Adam's wife. Adam called Eve, his wife. God presents Eve, but God does not tell Adam this is your wife. And I believe that's a model for modern-day relationships we should follow.

God can present someone before you, but never choose that person for you. It could be somebody God has wired and made to multiply to help you take dominion. Except for Hosea and Gomer, nowhere in the Scripture did God tell anybody to marry anybody. He eases Joseph's fears about Mary, the mother of Jesus, being pregnant, but Joseph had already chosen to marry Mary.

After God presents Eve to Adam, Adam makes the statement, "For this reason shall a man leave his father and mother and cleave to his wife." It's the first time we hear the word wife used because *Adam* called her that—not God.

Isaac and Rebekah

Abraham tells his servant, find my son, Isaac, a spouse. The father tells the servant to find the son a spouse and gives him parameters—make sure she's not a believer in false Gods. He says, find him somebody but make sure she's not an idol worshipper. Similar to the New Testament, which says, "Be ye not unequally yoked with unbelievers." That is the only thing God says about requirements for a spouse in the New Testament.

So he says find my son, Isaac, a spouse. Follow my parameters.

The servant goes out to look for a spouse and then prays, "God, lead me to the right person, and give me success, lead me to the right person." Then he creates parameters and said, "If this is the right person, let her offer a drink not only to me but my camels too." God never said that was a prerequisite. Abraham never said that was a prerequisite. That is the sign that the servant asked for to let him know who the right person was. The servant created parameters to help him identify the right person when he saw her. And I believe that supports us taking a similar approach in prayer.

For example, you could pray, "God, I know what your parameters are, but this is what I want. And the person I want, please let them have this character." We're not talking about possessions, but let them have this character.

He meets Rebekah, and she offers precisely what he asked for in prayer. He did not question her. She meets the parameters, offers a drink to him and the camels, and then the servant asks if she would marry Isaac.

She had a choice. She did not have to go; she went—sight unseen. So there was no initial physical attraction: she had not seen Isaac. There was nothing more than an offer, and she responded. She takes the offer. After that, she and Isaac meet and go into the marriage chamber. They married.

There was no dating. There was no, "God told me to marry you." The father decided when it was time for the son to get married and then gave the parameters for who he could and could not marry. Later, based on those parameters, the son chooses someone from a presentation.

And I believe God does the same thing with us. When the time is right, he'll lead us. He'll give us a choice. Once we know who we are—the son we are—and the Heavenly Father we have, we'll know the right parameters to ask for, and then we'll find somebody based on those parameters.

But don't give away the blueprint.

Notice, the servant did not forewarn Rebekah that if she gave water to the camels, he would choose her to be somebody's wife. He watched her character before he made the offer. People make the mistake of giving away the blueprint of what they want without waiting to watch the character of the individual they're getting to know.

And what that does is it gives the other individual an unfair advantage. Not to say that every individual tries to do it. But if there's somebody you're interested in, nine times out of ten, you will put your best foot forward and do what you know they want you to do—what you know is in their blueprint. So if they say they want a God-fearing man, the person they're seeing might start going to church more. If they say they want somebody who does Bible study, he might begin reading his Bible more. If they say they want somebody good with their kids, he might start playing with your kids more. If they say they want a great provider, he will show that he can provide.

However, the wise thing to do is to watch the character of the individual without giving them the blueprint to your heart. That way, you're not inadvertently manipulated even if they don't intend to do so.

But society today is in such a hyper pursuit of marriage, especially in the Church. Probably more in the Church than outside the Church. People in the Church are in such a hyper pursuit of marriage, whether it's because they want to have sex and not feel guilty, believe it releases their destiny, they want to have kids, or they think they can't be happy without marriage. I was that person. That's why I got married so many times so quickly.

There's such a pursuit of being married that most people look at every person they meet as a potential spouse rather than paying attention to their character. There's no entertainment of friendship because they're too busy trying to make a relationship. You hear people saying; I don't want to waste my time befriending people, rather than taking the time to know what type of person they're possibly marrying.

They are pursuing a relationship so strongly that they lose out on valuable connections because they don't think the person is a potential mate. That is the downside of pursuit. It can cause you to focus on the wrong things.

PART II: CONSIDERATIONS WHEN CHOOSING: WHAT I WISH I HAD KNOWN

5 DISCOVERY VERSUS PURSUIT

I consider myself a social guy. Whether I was in a relationship, the interactions between males and females always intrigued me. Growing up, I never had girlfriends, but I had female friends. And I would listen to their stories about pursuing males or males pursuing them. They had all kinds of stories about things they liked and didn't like. You learn a lot when people don't date you, but they tell you all their business about who they date.

As time has progressed, I've paid attention to how social media, online dating, and things of this nature have grown. Often on social media, both in and outside of the Church, you find many people giving their opinions, perspectives, and preferences on dating.

There are a monumental amount of women who share how they prefer a man pursue them. And they do it under the premise of, "A man who findeth a wife findeth a good thing." But as I reviewed interactions and responses, I realized that many of the women who post their preferences often get negative responses from the very men they're trying to instruct. Many men respond to their posts by commenting that it's a turnoff, or they are "doing too much."

I think the underlying issue is the Bible doesn't give many

examples of pursuing a woman. There aren't many biblical examples at all. I wonder if we have been missing the understanding of pursuit all these years.

> He that findeth a good woman, findeth a good thing; and of the Lord he shall draw up mirth (and he receiveth favour from the Lord). He that putteth away a good woman, putteth away a good thing; but he that holdeth (onto an) adulteress, is a fool and unwise. (Proverbs 18:22 Wycliffe Bible, WYC)

One of the Hebrew meanings of the word "findeth," is to discover, uncover, or come across. It's a different meaning than the way we typically think of finding as pursuing. It's almost saying if you *discover* a wife, a good woman, you have *uncovered* a good thing.

You don't always find something because you are pursuing it. Sometimes, you find something as you are going about the normal course of your day. Without sweat, you happen upon a dollar bill, a lost piece of jewelry, or another item. You weren't running after it, but you still found it. You weren't pursuing it, but you still found it—you discovered it.

We've turned marriage and selecting a mate into a pursuit instead of discovery. God presented Eve to Adam after Adam was already in purpose. God presented Eve to Adam. Adam did not send a search party throughout the garden to find his companion.

He was fulfilling his assignment, tending the garden, and taking dominion, and then God presented Eve to him. We can discover our mate as we're operating in purpose. But if we turn marriage into a pursuit of a man or woman, we ignore purpose.

If we embrace finding a mate as discovery during our journey, then we come across it while we're moving toward something else. It's part of the process of purpose. For example, while I was building my business, I met somebody, or while I was serving in church, or taking my kids to daycare, I met somebody. When the focus is on purpose, you don't have to chase people, follow, or hunt them down on social media. No, none of that is the case when you pursue your purpose and not people.

People may think "dear future wife" or "dear future husband" posts are cute, but it's advertising. Some people do it for others to see them and to put themselves out there. They are trying to be discovered. But if instead, they would operate in purpose, the way Adam did, they would come across their mate and discover them along their journey. Along the lane they're already driving in, they'll discover their spouse. They'll discover the person who's appropriate to build with them.

When you do it this way, it takes away the mad pursuit. You don't feel bothered when a man doesn't pursue you, or a woman doesn't pursue you. Why? Rather than chasing someone or being chased, the goal is to fulfill your purpose. A chase indicates that something may or may not be caught.

Boaz woke up one night and found Ruth lying at his feet. He wasn't pursuing her, and she wasn't pursuing him. She was following Naomi's instructions. Boaz was even going to allow another relative to marry Ruth. But because Ruth served her mother-in-law, working in the fields, and following her instructions, Boaz discovered her—just as she was.

Everyone knew Ruth was a Moabite and a widow. She hid nothing nor did she write "Dear Boaz" posts. She was willing to journey with her mother-in-law to follow purpose, and as a result, Boaz found her.

6 FALSE ADVERTISEMENT

When I met Stacy (I have changed her name to protect her identity), we often talked on the phone. The intent from the jump was a relationship that led to marriage. My focus was not on friendship; it was on a romantic relationship. So when I met her, everything about our conversation was regarding relationship-type stuff.

I remember sharing with her my desires regarding a relationship, and what characteristics and behavioral habits I wanted in a spouse. I told her three things were important to me. One of those things was marrying a woman who cooked. I needed a woman who cooked because that was something that I grew up seeing my mother do. My mother cooked every Sunday; no matter what, we had Sunday dinner. We rarely went out on Sunday because Sunday was family dinner. One of my favorite dinners was white rice, gravy, and roast with green beans. Nobody could cook it like my mama. And if she didn't cook roast, she fried chicken. She would cook white rice, green beans, and fried chicken, and that was the perfect dinner for me.

So in response, Stacy would say, "Well, I love to cook. I cook all the time for me and my household, so that's no problem for me."

The first time Stacy invited me to her townhouse, it was very casual. The plan was to hang out and watch a few movies, and then I would go home. But when I got there, Stacy made the most amazing fried chicken, rice, and green beans. I mean, it was amazing, and I felt like, oh my goodness, this woman really cooks. She cooked this dinner, and she had pulled out a table and put it right in front of the TV so I could sit there and watch the TV.

She served my plate. I had mentioned that was also important to me because I grew up in a traditional home. My mother served my dad his plate first, out of respect, and out of honor. We all had the food, but my daddy ate first. And so that was something I shared was important to me.

That night, she served my plate, sat it right on the table in front of me, asked if there was something I wanted to drink, and I was astonished. It dumbfounded me that there was a woman who literally did what my mother did.

I would never forget that night. I thought I finally found someone who would do these things. In my previous relationships, my spouses didn't cook. I knew how to cook, so I didn't mind doing it. But finally, it was just nice to have somebody who would do it. I mean, this is what I was looking for in a spouse. I shared that this is what I was looking for, and here she is doing it. How amazing is that? She must be the one.

What's funny is that after we got married, I started to note that it wasn't a regular occurrence. It wasn't even a regular habit because it appeared it was a struggle for her to cook. Her response was either, "Oh, I'm tired from working," or "There's too much going on." Not to say that those weren't valid reasons, but cooking wasn't the norm.

I realized that it's possible that maybe just maybe, she did that because she knew that's what I wanted even though that wasn't who she was on the regular. That wasn't her normal behavior.

Maybe she presented what she had expected she would do on the regular, or wanted to show that wasn't a problem, but that just wasn't who she was. Unfortunately, I made an assumption and had an expectation based on what she showed me on one or two occasions, but that wasn't the reality of the situation.

Now conversely, I realize I did the same thing. She expressed that it was very important to her that whatever man she was with was not jealous, but understood that she and her child's father had a great relationship, a friendship. And even though they didn't work out as a couple, they were still cordial. She understood that I had challenges with people being friends with their exes because of my past two relationships.

But I understood, and I told her, "I'm not a jealous guy. I'm not in competition with anybody. I'm very secure in my position, and that's not an issue." When I met the guy, he seemed like a nice guy. So I was like. "This will not be a problem because I'm a secure man. I don't have those issues. I've dealt with my previous experiences in relationships. I've come to terms with having been cheated on with exes; it won't be a problem."

However, very early, about three or four months into the relationship, I realized how unsettled I was with their relationship. I was very unsettled with the level of communication that they had; their friendliness troubled me deeply.

I was very unsettled with the demeanor and the companionship that they still maintained. If he ever needed something, she was quick to assist. If he ever couldn't get off of work on time to pick up their child, she was quick to assist. And I felt that that was overstepping because I married her. It wasn't her job to do things for him as a wife would. They were just coparents.

My background with my children's mother was very different. We didn't get along at all. We barely talked, and even to this day, we have a strained relationship. It's not intentional; it's just never been any other way. So, I had a real challenge with accepting the level of communication, friendship, and interaction they had.

Even though I told her I was secure in the beginning, I was so insecure that I began to compare myself to him physically because I felt they had a sexual attraction and not just a friendship. He was a little more muscular than me, and he dressed differently than me. I compared myself and started to work out more.

I went to the gym more because I thought, maybe, if I was more muscular, more fit, and more like what she seemed attracted to, she would respond to me differently. Perhaps she would put how I felt about their friendship first.

I was truly jealous, and I can't be sure if it was because I was paying attention to their demeanors and interactions, or if it stemmed from unresolved issues from past relationships. I always felt like me just being me was never good enough.

I falsely presented myself. I thought I was a man I hadn't become yet. I wasn't secure. I wasn't firm in who I was, and because of that, I sold myself as something I hadn't yet become.

That's the danger with false advertisement. Just like any product you buy from the store, once you advertise yourself as one thing, only for someone to discover that you're not, people want to return to the sender. They want to return for a refund. We have to be honest about who we are, so we don't advertise ourselves falsely.

While dating, and even at the beginning of a marriage, we usually present the best version of ourselves—not necessarily who and what we are and do regularly. We present who we're striving to be, or what we believe the other person wants.

You can also present a false version of yourself when you don't realize or accept your deficiencies. For example, I did not realize how much I deflected responsibility and how much previous relationships had hurt me.

Before my third marriage ended, I had two hundred twenty-two church members. Keep in mind, she and I had legally separated but still lived in the same house together. I knew she had somebody, and I also had someone else. I was ready to end the marriage.

It was December 31, 2017. I told her, "You know what? This is not going to work. I'm done." I already had someone else and would move out. In response, that girl dressed up in the dress she had on when we first went out. She was like, "Whatever it is, we can work it out." That got me. So, we both cried and agreed to work it out. We tried to move forward.

But deep down, she couldn't start fresh. She couldn't wipe the slate clean. So she was having secret meetings with the Church, telling people that I had cheated and taken money from the Church. We didn't need to take money from the Church because we were making $40,000 a month from three successful daycares. We had a great house and great cars; we needed nothing. We were doing great financially, but she was having secret meetings. We had an eleven thousand square foot church building. The Church was exploding after just three years.

But after her meetings, I went from two hundred twenty members to twenty-five in six weeks. When I found out what was going on, it broke me. I said, "'f' God, 'f' all y'all, I'm done with the church. I'm not doing this anymore." But rather than accept responsibility for the part I played, I deflected. Legally separated or not, we were still married. I shouldn't have been involved with anyone regardless of what I thought she was doing or with whom. Biblically, I didn't have a right to be with anyone outside my marriage.

To know who you are, you have to know the areas where you are deficient.

I deflected, which means I didn't accept responsibility for my actions. While I seemed like I had everything under control, I passed off blame in so many areas. I wanted to be the head, but I didn't want the responsibility.

So with false advertisements, we have to make sure we are who we say we are. If a woman is dating a man, she can cook dinner for him once or twice to imply that she cooks all the time. But if she really doesn't cook, that could be a huge issue. Remember, Stacy presented herself as someone who would cook often, but in the years we were together, she probably cooked twelve times. I didn't pay attention as I should have. But for me, home dinners on Sunday were important. Once again, this was a false advertisement, and we both did it.

Also, we have to make sure we're not presenting ourselves as humble when really, we're arrogant. I was superarrogant because I was the youngest pastor in my jurisdiction with a church that size, successful businesses, a great house, and cars. I would say, "Oh, it's the Lord," but in the back of my mind, I was like, "Yeah, I'm doing well." I thought I was humble, but I was arrogant. We present ourselves to be this best version of ourselves and never really take the time to discover who we are—that includes discovering our deficiencies.

I didn't find out who I was until I went to counseling for six months. Every day during the sessions, I would talk about how everybody else did me wrong and how hurt I was. How could everybody be mad at me when my ex did what she did? Everybody in her family was cheating on their spouses, but they wanted to blast me for what I did. Then one day, I went to counseling and said, "You know what, though, it's my fault. I was wrong, and people wouldn't have had anything to talk about if I didn't do what I did." That was the first time in my life that I accepted full responsibility without deflecting. It released me. I felt so good!

There is power in transparency—in being our real selves—even when being exposed is painful. When you confess your faults, you take away the power of the enemy. Jacob, the trickster, learned this lesson when he wrestled with God. It wasn't until Jacob called his name, confessing his trickster nature, that God changed his name.

> Then Jacob was left alone; and a Man wrestled with him until the breaking of day. [25] Now when He saw that He did not prevail against him, He touched the socket of his hip; and the socket of Jacob's hip was out of joint as He wrestled with him. [26] And He said, "Let Me go, for the day breaks." But he said, "I will not let You go unless You bless me!" [27] So He said to him, "What *is* your name?" He said, "Jacob." [28] And He said, "Your name shall no longer be called Jacob, but Israel; for you have struggled with God and with men, and have prevailed." [29] Then Jacob asked, saying, "Tell *me* Your name, I pray." And He said, "Why *is* it *that* you ask about My name?" And He blessed him there. [30] So Jacob called the name of the place: "For I have seen God face to face, and my life is preserved." [31] Just as he crossed over Penuel the sun rose on him, and he limped on his hip. (Genesis 32:24-31 NKJV)

Jacob was a heal-grabber, swindler, and trickster. It took Jacob admitting who he was for God to change his name. You have to know yourself to assess who's a good fit for you. That includes knowing the good, bad, and ugly of who you are. God will give you a choice, and to choose effectively, be honest with yourself about your strengths and your weaknesses.

Take responsibility for who you are. Don't false advertise. There may be things in your background that have negatively influenced you. Take responsibility for those things and work on them. In the next chapter, we'll discuss influences from our past that can impact our future relationships if we don't take responsibility.

7 UNDERSTANDING INFLUENCES

I married my second wife quickly. I didn't spend much time learning her family history and background. However, I received a clear view once we moved in with my in-laws (her family). I realized that we had very different family backgrounds. They attended church, but their lifestyle outside of the Church was so different from my own.

Everybody in their house drank alcohol regularly. That was not the case in my family, and I had little experience with drinking alcohol. I rarely drank, if at all. So living in their home was an adjustment.

Eight people were living in the house, including one particular aunt who drank daily. Aunt Jane could do a twenty-four pack of beer in a single day. On several occasions, I saw Aunt Jane passed out on the patio from drinking. My mother-in-law, father-in-law, brothers-in-law, and my spouse all drank regularly.

Living in that home gave me some perspective. I learned some things about family differences. Everybody has different vices, habits, morals, and culture.

After certain infractions in our marriage occurred, I picked up a habit that ultimately was a coping mechanism to deal with what was happening. I started drinking. I don't know if it was because of the normalcy of the drinking situation in the house. But I dare say, drinking being so commonplace around me influenced who I was as a person. It affected my behavior.

Soon, I was drinking a bottle of rum a day without fail. I wouldn't get intoxicated. However, I would have a drink to relax and go to sleep. And that became my daily routine. I will never forget, my wife at the time pulled me aside and said, "Hey 'E,' I think you're becoming an alcoholic." I replied, "Nah, not me. I don't even get faded. Yeah, I drank a whole bottle, but I don't even get faded." She said, "That's the problem. You don't even realize how much alcohol you're drinking, and it's not even having an impact on you."

From that moment, I regulated and cut back—cut off almost completely—any drinking. It had become a vice I used when I got depressed. It was a vice for when I didn't know how to cope. I had become influenced by my surroundings.

That is not the only situation that can influence you. Sometimes the mere presence of people can influence you. My third marriage is an example.

My third wife would change when she was around certain people. She was very quiet at home, cool, calm, affectionate, and kind. She was always respectful and never harsh with words; she was never rude to me in the home at the beginning of the marriage. However, the dynamics changed when she was around her sisters and mother. She'd be harsher; she'd be a little sharper with her words. In my opinion, every woman in her family "wore the pants" in her home. Her demeanor towards me changed when she was around them.

Most of the men in her family were quieter. I won't say submissive, but they were more apt to please their spouse or girlfriend. It was not always healthy, but it was undoubtedly the way they attempted to keep the peace. The problem was that it *prevented healthy decisions because they would do what the spouse, wife, or girlfriend wanted to keep them from going off.*

The more we were around them, the more she would expect the same from me. There were many arguments where I made statements like, "I'm not your daddy." Or, "I'm not your brother-in-law." "You're not your sister; you're not going to talk to me the way they talk to them." "You're not your mom. This is not going to happen in this house. That might work for them, but that's not going to work for us."

The influences of family culture and environments impact the person you marry. Therefore, you must pay attention to their upbringing and the attitudes of their siblings and parents. Both her parents had children from previous marriages. Although they got remarried to each other, in my opinion, the interaction between them was as if they were still in a relationship with their coparent. They were too close to their coparents! There should have been a tangible difference between their relationship as husband and wife and the relationship they had with their coparents.

Had I paid attention to that influence, it would have explained the dynamics of the relationship that my wife had with her child's father. It was normal for them to have conversations that I would consider inappropriate. It was normal for them to have meetups, of which even I wasn't aware. It was normal to them, but if I had paid attention to the influences of her family, I would have recognized the potential challenges that had arisen in our relationship. I would have prepared.

Assessing influences is crucial because knowingly and unknowingly, people inherit behaviors. We become the product of our surroundings. Famous motivational speaker, Jim Rohn, said, "We are the average of the five people we spend the most time with."

> *"We are the average of the five people we spend the most time with."* —Jim Rohn

Culture and upbringing can cloud your perspective regarding a potential spouse. They have an influence on your behavior and the person you choose. Everyone can inherit behaviors from their family even if they don't realize it. Sometimes, you have made normalcy out of dysfunction because of your upbringing. As a result, you see life—and your potential spouse—from the lens of dysfunction. Therefore, you do not see well when choosing a spouse. I didn't see well with my third spouse.

Conversely, you can misjudge someone based upon your upbringing. For example, my parents have been together my entire life. In thirty-seven years, I've never witnessed them argue, and for most people, that is uncommon. Thus, when I encountered arguments or disagreements in my own relationships, I instantly felt as if they were doomed because my parents never argued. We really have to take time to observe and assess why we are the way we are.

Abraham and his sons show us an example of inherited behaviors.

Abraham told him Pharaoh that his wife was his sister (Genesis 12:12-17). Abraham's son, Isaac, told Abimelech that his wife, Rebekah, was his sister. And Jacob, Isaac's son—well, he took it to another level.

Isaac learned to lie from his upbringing with his father, who loved God, followed God's direction, and had a godly culture, but still passed down some ungodly characteristics. Abraham had an issue with lying, and his son Isaac did the same thing when confronted with a similar situation with his spouse. What was next? Jacob, Isaac's son, not only lies about his spouse but also deceives his father to get the blessing.

You cannot ignore the fact that you can be god-fearing, god-serving, and god-hearing and still have character issues that were passed down from generation to generation. These issues influence your behavior in a relationship.

That applies to both people in a potential relationship. Not only do you have to watch out for your tendencies but also your potential spouse's. How you were both raised and the dynamics of the households that influenced you are so important.

That's not to say that everybody will be like the generation that came before them. But we understand that the Scripture says to train up a child in the way they should go, and they will not depart from it. That also applies in the reverse or converse. If you train them badly, they will inherit bad traits—the bad can also stick with them. They can carry the same bad character habits into marriage.

That doesn't mean that people can't be free from their past. Yes, people can break generational curses, and bad character habits can change. However, when dysfunction is all you know, it will be normal and acceptable to you. If your father hit your mother, you might think it is normal to see your mother get hit. You might think it is normal to hit your spouse. If your grandmother used extreme measures to correct you, it wouldn't be farfetched for you to do the same.

Now, my father loves me and has never abused me. But whenever I became disrespectful, my daddy used to say something to me on those rare occasions. He used to say, "Boy, I'll kill you." Based on his tone, I knew he didn't mean it literally. But after I had my children, I integrated that phrase into my habits. When my son would get smart, I used to say, "Boy, I will kill you right now." Well, one day, my son went to school and relayed what I said to his teacher. It caused me all kinds of problems with the school. There are inherited behaviors that we can repeat and consider normal without recognizing their toxicity.

A few years back, I owned three daycares. From that experience, I learned that the government now considers some things our parents did for correction as child abuse. And it probably was child abuse then. Start paying attention to the habits of the culture and habits of the parents of your spouse or potential spouse. Here are some questions you should ask yourself and carefully observe for answers:

- How do the men treat the women in the family?
- How do the women treat the men in the family?
- Do both parents work?
- Who's the disciplinary?
- Who cooks?
- Who cleans?
- What are their spending habits?
- What's the relationship like with their children?
- Who's the head of the home?
- Who submits to who?
- Who's the spiritual head?
- What are their religious customs?

Be mindful; if you're not a submissive man, then you probably can't be with someone who is used to seeing overly submissive men in their family. In my third marriage, my in-laws had a string of overly submissive men. Now, I realize all of my former spouses were used to seeing submissive men. That created contention when it came time for decision making. Conversely, if you're a woman who likes gentler or submissive men, you must be very intentional about observing his upbringing. Otherwise, butting heads may be unavoidable.

Ahab is an example of what I call an "overly submissive man." His life reveals what can happen when men have inherited overly submissive behaviors.

Jezebel and Ahab

Jezebel has a bad reputation. Often, we focus on Jezebel-like behaviors in families, but we don't deal with Ahab-like behaviors. However, Jezebel can only thrive when Ahab is present. Jezebel only thrives when Ahab is weak and will not stand for what is right. But if you kill Ahab, Jezebel dies. Meaning, if you can get a man to stand firm on his faith and his belief, then Jezebel will either leave or destroy herself. She can't survive. All it takes is someone willing to stand on the word of God in a particular issue, and Jezebel cannot survive.

But as long as an Ahab is fearful of what a Jezebel might do, she will always promote him publicly but control him privately. She will emasculate him behind closed doors or publicly embarrass him. But she will always display her strength. Sometimes, she will display strength and get him to submit to please her, in response to a sin he's committed because sin diminishes dominion. When you give up dominion, give up your rightful place through sin, and your countenance diminishes in front of the person you're with, you hand over the authority. That is why abstinence from sin is so important.

So many relationships become imbalanced because of a spouse's sin or offense. Because of sin, they yield authority as an exchange for forgiveness. For example, someone may cheat on their spouse. And as a result, they inadvertently do whatever the spouse wants as a recompense. Those behaviors inadvertently birth a Jezebel spirit in the home. The offender will do whatever the offended wants to foster peace and happiness. Thus, it empowers the offended to lead from an emotional place, which often results in bad decision-making.

Ahab allowed Jezebel to run the kingdom behind closed doors, and he was nothing more than a face. When this happens in the home, it creates a skewed perspective, a perspective different from what God intended for the family unit. Instead of God's biblical precedent for leadership in the home, they run things from an unauthorized place. God wants to deal with Ahab's in the homes, so we can build our homes based upon biblical precedent and not based upon negative experiences, feelings, emotions, revenge, wrath, or malice.

In marriage, dealing with Ahab requires the man of the house to be strong enough to stand for what is right, despite his fear of the response of his spouse. A wife can become a Jezebel inadvertently, purely because she's embracing a role that's not designed for her. If she's trying to control the kingdom (the family) by manipulation, she's not in her rightful place. That's only in marriage because the Scripture says the husband is the head of the wife; it didn't say all men are the head of all women.

Conversely, men can embrace a Jezebel spirit by using manipulation to control their wife. Often, men use finances and other provisions to control their spouse. God said that the husband was the "head," but he never stated that the couple had the same mind. A wife's submission does not mean a submission of her mind, will, and emotions; but a Godly submission as the word of God instructs. Relationships built biblically shouldn't need manipulation to function or progress. It is the responsibility of each party to observe and prayerfully consider the behaviors of their potential mate to avoid these situations.

Influences of Family Culture

Pay attention to the family culture and behaviors of parents. We have to understand the dynamics of people's upbringing, including how they deal with money. What were their financial habits? What were they used to?

One of my exes was used to her parents maxing out credit cards so they could have presents under the Christmas tree. They were on government assistance, but would max out credit cards so all the kids could have lots of presents under the tree. Afterward, they would spend the rest of the year trying to pay off the debt from the gifts.

That can be a point of conflict for somebody like me whose parents bought us each three gifts because they would not go into debt over Christmas. We got three gifts, and that was good enough. Further, birthdays were not a huge deal to us because my parents' motto was, "You should be grateful the Lord allowed you to live." We'd typically have a homemade birthday cake, and we may have gotten one birthday gift. So for me, birthdays were never events to celebrate. That was problematic when the time came to celebrate my children's or spouse's birthday.

Even now, birthday celebrations are a challenge for me because I don't see a need to "go all out" and spend lots of money. When my kids have a birthday, I rarely do anything big or plan a huge party. I often jokingly say, "My kids are blessed if they even get a birthday cake." And it's all because of my upbringing. We have to understand those influences because they can make dynamics in the house challenging.

We have to know who we are to assess what we want, and more so, what we need.

Influences of Past Relationships

I had to come to grips with how my past relationships had influenced me. I had insecurities and scars that would impact any future relationship negatively. It was so crucial for me to be honest in this area. Sometimes, people don't like to talk about their hurts, but if we are not honest with ourselves, we will create a pattern of recurring issues and broken relationships because we do not own who we are.

Because I was honest, I was adamant that my current wife have no communication with her child's father.

I was so hurt by my previous relationships that on my list of twenty-four things that I wanted in a woman, one of my requests to God was that if my next wife had a child, she had to have no communication with her baby daddy. She could have a kid, but the father had to be absent. Matter of fact, the child couldn't even be younger than my children. And did I mention, the father had to be absent? I didn't want any access from a prior relationship. I prayed for an absent daddy because all three of my exes had cheated on me with their exes or children's father.

Ironically, my current wife had minimal communication with her child's father due to incarceration. All he could do was call now and then. And when we got married, he was clear across the country. When he got out, there was no issue because there was no tangible influence. The Lord knew what he was doing; because he knew, I couldn't take it.

Past issues of rejection, feelings of abandonment, and past relationships that don't have closure are all influences you must deal with before entering a new relationship. Some people feel like they have to continue to have conversations with past partners after they're married to figure out what happened. But marriage requires a higher level of wisdom. Not bringing past relationships to a close can lead to temptation and cheating. I share my story about cheating and temptation in the next chapter.

PART III: MAKE SURE YOU'RE HEALED

8 CHEATING AND TEMPTATION

There I was, standing around the corner from our bedroom, and I heard her yelling.

"How come you didn't tell me?" she yelled while sobbing and crying. "You got her pregnant, how come you didn't tell me?"

"Who is she talking to?" I wondered. "Is she talking to her brother? Maybe her brother-in-law?"

"You were man enough to do it," she said. "How come you weren't man enough to tell me? How long were you going to keep this from me?"

Then, she said his name. She was talking to her child's father, yelling and sobbing on the phone because he had gotten another woman pregnant. I watched her cry, scream, and yell.

"How come you didn't tell me you got another woman pregnant?" she exclaimed. She hung up the phone.

"Why are you crying?" I asked methodically.

"Can you be my friend right now?" she replied.

"Yeah," I said.

"Well, I always thought I would be the only one, and I feel like she's taking my place."

I rubbed her hair as she lay in my lap and cried about her child's father getting another woman pregnant. I watched my wife cry about another man having a baby with another woman.

Thoughts of all the inappropriate text messages they exchanged, and times people called me to tell me they were sleeping together, bombarded my mind. At that moment, I knew it was all true. They were deeply involved. No one responds the way she did unless there's a deep emotional connection. Inwardly, I decided the relationship was over.

In response, I began to blur boundaries. I developed friendships with women—not necessarily sexual—but they became emotional support. As a result, my wife and I were seldom intimate. In my mind, I knew things were going on with her, and that her attachment to her child's father was inordinate.

Even when we were intimate, she'd complain that there was no passion. It made me feel insufficient, like I couldn't even please my spouse. Even when I'd try new things, it didn't change the complaint. What was I doing wrong? Maybe I needed to be more muscular like him. Maybe it wouldn't matter.

Eventually, I didn't want to be intimate with her, but that also pushed me to seek intimacy elsewhere. Self-inflicted or not, I wasn't getting intimacy from her, and it created a problem. I found intimacy elsewhere.

I filed legal separation and got a place to stay. I had become so disconnected from my wife; I was comfortable engaging in a relationship with someone else. I lived in a constant place of mental conflict. Here I am, pastoring one of the fasting growing churches in my city and denomination. However, I found myself so deeply in a relationship with another woman that I justified it because it filled voids in my life and emotions—voids that had been present a long time. Despite how sinful it was, it was meeting real needs in my life. This wasn't a test from God or a trick of the enemy. It was a temptation that was birthed from inside me. The Scripture says temptation comes from the lusts and desires of our hearts.

> Let no man say when he is tempted, I am tempted of God: for God cannot be tempted with evil, neither tempteth he any man: [14] But every man is tempted, when he is drawn away of his own lust, and enticed. [15] Then when lust hath conceived, it bringeth forth sin: and sin, when it is finished, bringeth forth death. (James 1:13-15 KJV)

What I was receiving from that extra-marital relationship was meeting real desires. The problem was, the wrong person was meeting my needs. Temptations will cause you to dishonor your marriage if you don't have the right boundaries.

From experience, I've observed a few things that can lead an individual to cheat. One of them is an emotional disconnect or lack of emotional intimacy and connection in the relationship. A lack of connection can include: no communication, no flirting, no touching, or a lack of feeling wanted. When any of that takes place, a spouse can seek those things elsewhere. Remember, there's always something lurking outside the walls of your city. Lack of communication wears away at boundaries, and eventually, the walls fall.

A lack of sexual intimacy can also lead someone to cheat. If a spouse expresses a need for sexual intimacy, the other spouse must meet the need. Every couple should discuss sexual needs in counseling before marriage, and sexual interactions should not lessen because spouses have gotten comfortable in their covenant. Often, we disregard our spouse's need for sexual intimacy. We write it off as being shallow, fleshy, or superficial, but it's not the job of the spouse to question whether it's a valid need. A spouse's job is to meet that need because they vowed to put their mate's needs before their own.

> The wife hath not power of her own body, but the husband: and likewise also the husband hath not power of his own body, but the wife. [5] Defraud ye not one the other, except it be with consent for a time, that ye may give yourselves to fasting and prayer; and come together again, that Satan tempt you not for your incontinency. [6] But I speak this by permission, and not of commandment. (1 Corinthians 7:4-6 KJV)

An excellent way to get your spouse to stop telling you what they need is to punish them for expressing what they need. Also, not responding to their expression and not attempting to meet the need that they've expressed can discourage them from talking. Why should they continuously express what they need if you will not do it; or if they will be punished for it later? Not having sexual needs met and not feeling safe to talk about it can lead the most god-fearing person to cheat. They will seek fulfillment of their needs elsewhere.

Another reason people cheat is a lack of peace in a home.

> Better to dwell in a corner of a housetop, than in a house shared with a contentious woman. (Proverbs 21:9 NKJV)

Constant contention can lead someone to cheat and move outside the home. The purpose of a covenant is to bring peace, not constant arguing and frustration. The covenant should make you better. When it's clear that dysfunction and endless arguments have taken over the marriage, people seek peace and joy elsewhere—especially men. Never underestimate the importance of having peace in your home.

For a man, other than respect, the best currency is peace. If a man doesn't have peace, he doesn't want to be there. That is why a lot of men will stay out late and take extra trips somewhere else because they don't want to deal with the arguing at home.

Regarding respect, if a man feels his spouse views him in a diminished way, he will seek places and people who honor him. Men always want to feel like "the man." They always desire honor, even though they do not realize that a lack of honor probably comes from their misbehavior. Regardless, a man just wants his spouse to honor and respect him.

As an example, for most men, even if they don't want you, they feel threatened when somebody else wants you or you want somebody else because they want to be on top. They want to be the head. They want to be the most important thing in their spouse's life next to God. God designed husbands to be the head.

When they feel like they're not their spouse's head because of contention, they hold their heads down. They want somebody to lift their head or to motivate them with the reassurance that they are a good man. Men will present themselves as something grand to someone else, knowing well and good they were horrible to their spouse.

With cheating, we have to be honest with ourselves and ask the hard questions.

I believe men cheat when there is a lack of something, whether respect, peace, self-confidence, or a lack of confidence in the relationship's longevity. A lack of self-esteem or trust in the relationship can lead to fear. They may fear the relationship will end, or that they are not enough. Fear can cause people to cheat. And men have to ask the hard questions to own up to their fears' contribution to cheating.

It is my opinion that it's easier for women to cheat when they've lost respect and honor for their husbands. They feel like their man is less than what he is. I think it's easier for a woman to cheat when her man has shown himself to be weak and not the head.

I also think women innately want a head because I believe that's how God wired them. So while they might like control, especially alpha women or women used to operating outside of God's design, I believe they still innately want someone to be the head. And that's when they look for someone they can't control but will give them attention and make them feel wanted, sexy, and loved.

When a man does not take the initiative and lead his woman to a place of paradise, she may cheat. Adam's job was to maintain a paradise for Eve. When paradise is ruined, wives want somebody who will bring them paradise again. They want somebody who will make them feel like Eve. They desire somebody who will make them feel like they are the most important thing in their Garden of Eden. And I believe that leads them to cheat. I think it happens for women first emotionally and then turns physical, and it happens first physically for men and then turns emotional.

Don't get me wrong; women want peace, and emotional and sexual intimacy too. For women, I believe cheating is emotional before it gets physical. So a husband needs to meet his wife's emotional needs.

Men must also understand the importance of leading in all areas. I find it interesting how men want to lead in most areas, but some men complain about the lack of initiative their spouse may take for sexual intimacy. If men would consistently minister to the emotional needs of their spouse, when they initiate sexual intimacy, they'd be amazed at the response they'd receive from their wives. When women feel safe and protected by the one that covers them, they will follow you to the ends of the earth. That applies literally and sexually.

I hope that if you understand some contributors to cheating, you can use the knowledge to protect your marriage and prevent cheating from happening in your relationship. I realize that other reasons may lead a spouse to cheat. However, if you can maintain an emotional connection, sexual intimacy, peace, and respect, you will be well on your way to preventing cheating in your marriage.

Now, some cheat regardless of the state of their marriage. They cheat when things are wrong and even when nothing is wrong. And that is why we discuss forgiveness in the next chapter.

9 FORGIVENESS

After the separation, we mutually agreed to give our marriage one last shot. We moved back into the house, and both promised that we would forgive and start fresh. For once, I forgave holding nothing against my wife. But it seemed my forgiveness looked different from hers. I wanted to live like there was a clean slate. For her, it was difficult. She couldn't let go of the emotions associated with the things that had transpired between the two of us. The first few months were a challenge. We stayed in the same room, trying to work out our marriage.

By the third month, she said, "I think we need to separate again."

I had already let go of my apartment, and I brought my children back into the situation after a lengthy court battle. They had witnessed things that should not have happened in the home. So they were already hurt and seriously impacted, but I decided I would live in forgiveness and not hold it against her. After her request to separate again, I moved to another room in the house. Even then, forgiveness was still at the forefront of my mind. Forgiveness is a choice. You "for-" give; you give it before they deserve it.

In those last three months of our marriage, I knew that she was still unfaithful. I knew she sometimes went to places she wasn't supposed to with people she should not have. I knew about the out-of-state rendezvouses. But I had committed to forgiving, and I was no longer angry.

I had been going to counseling, and it helped me understand that to forgive, I also had to admit the areas where I had failed. I had to take responsibility for my contribution to the state of the marriage. Counseling helped me see that no matter what someone else does, I have to be accountable for myself. When I began to hold myself responsible, I became more remorseful for the things I had done to catapult my spouse's wrong choices.

Even though I forgave, time proved that the relationship wasn't reconcilable, not because I didn't want it to be, but things had progressed beyond what she was willing or able to forgive. Forgiveness has the potential to lead to reconciliation in a marriage, but that only happens by choice. Forgiveness can facilitate absolving someone of punishment, but it doesn't always mean they resume the same placement in your life.

When one spouse breaks trust, the other spouse has to be honest, seek God, and decide if they can receive their spouse back in the same placement, fully embracing reconciliation. It's easier said than done.

> Then came Peter to him, and said, Lord, how oft shall my brother sin against me, and I forgive him? till seven times? [22] Jesus saith unto him, I say not unto thee, Until seven times: but, Until seventy times seven. (Matthew 18:21-22 KJV)

For true forgiveness in a relationship to manifest, brace yourself and go beyond lofty ideals, especially after infidelity. Peter underestimated the capacity necessary to maintain a forgiving relationship. Like Peter, many betrayed spouses thought they could move past it. But they just could not let go of the hurt and pain.

Ask yourself, "Can I really walk this process of forgiveness out?" Look at the situation and assess if it is possible to forgive wholly, understanding that your spouse doesn't earn forgiveness. You give it when it's not earned or deserved. You cannot force it. The offended person has to offer it willingly. There are big problems when you want to make people earn forgiveness, which is impossible.

It is also impossible for the person who hurt you to heal you. They are the offender. They cannot heal you. There is only one person who can heal you, and that is God. To put the pressure on the offender for your healing is improper because you're setting them up for an unfair expectation—one that nobody can meet and setting yourself up for hurt again. If God can't fix it, no one can. It surely can't be the person who hurt you. It's impossible.

Nor can any future companion or spouse heal you. They're not capable or qualified, nor should they handle the wound. They can help nurse you or nurture you. They can lead you to the Father God, who is the only one that can heal you. But no one else is qualified to heal you.

You have to know who to go to for healing, and it surely isn't the person who hurt you. You can ruin a potentially good relationship by placing the burden of recovery on them. Just because they are willing to endure, doesn't mean you should force them to do so. If you're not careful, you can hurt them. And hurt people, hurt people.

In the forgiveness process, we have to evaluate if we are, in fact, capable of letting go of the need to punish the person who hurt us. You can't say, I forgive you, and still want to punish them. You can't want them to earn the right to be your spouse again, or earn the right to respect or trust again as your spouse. They still need to regain trust. But we have to be honest with ourselves and admit whether we can or cannot move beyond the offense to heal; because forgiveness is a decision, but healing is a process.

I don't believe that anyone should try to rebuild a relationship while there are still open wounds. Meaning, if you're still bleeding, feeling anger, wrath, or desire for vengeance, you should not engage in romantic behavior until that's resolved. You risk rubbing, irritating, and exposing your wounds prematurely. It may rip the scar and cause you to bleed again. Wounds that go unaddressed for too long become infectious. And infections that go without the right medication spread quickly. For example, if you go to the movies together and there's a cheating scene in the film, it may set you off. It's just not healthy.

There needs to be some time for evaluation. It needs to be long enough for emotions to have died down, so you can evaluate whether you want the relationship, and can and will forgive. The offender also needs to evaluate if they will wait and endure the forgiveness process.

Sometimes the spouse is more capable of recognizing the other person's capacity to forgive because they observe them from the outside. For example, my wife probably knows my ability to forgive her more than I do. My blind spots do not cripple her assessment of my capacity. She knows what I can and cannot handle. Even when we think we know, sometimes the spouse knows better. Sometimes, it will be the responsibility of the person who's in the covenant to recognize what's best for the other person.

We have to assess the condition of the heart. If the spouse's heart has gotten hard, and they are unwilling to let God soften it, there's nothing you can do. You cannot change their choice. You can pray and wait, and that doesn't mean you have to end the relationship. But you may have to remove yourself until they realize or fully embrace forgiveness. In the meantime, forgive yourself.

Forgive Yourself

Recently, I was elevated to the office of Overseer, and getting a lot of congratulations, both personally and online. I got one particular message from a brother in Christ through Facebook Messenger. It started with congratulations on where God had brought me from and how amazing it was that God had opened up new doors. But then, the conversation shifted. He said, "You know, I want to share this with you as a brother. People are still talking about you; your name is still out there in the streets." He talked about how he was at his church, and somebody was asking, "Who is this pastor that married four times, and cheated on his ex?" He also said, while he was at Wawa, he heard two people talking about this pastor who recently remarried for the fourth time.

For a few moments, I experienced a weight of guilt and disappointment. I felt like the good deeds I had done didn't matter—people would always bring up the negative I'd done. That is why you have to make sure you not only walk in forgiveness for others but also forgive yourself.

Paul makes the statement, "Oh wretched man that I am, who shall deliver me from this body of death?" He then answers, "I thank God through Jesus Christ our Lord." (Romans 7:24-25a KJV) Jesus delivers. Remember, all of us are wretched in some area, or were wretched in some area. But when you repent and ask God to forgive you that forgiveness extends over every situation and transgression. You should no longer hold your head down.

How people treat you after they say they have forgiven you, is contingent upon how you treat yourself. If you walk with your head held down, if you walk with inward displeasure for yourself, people will emulate that same behavior. Make sure you have forgiven yourself, so people see you properly as someone walking in victory.

If you genuinely believe that God has forgiven you, act like it—conduct yourself like it. Don't let the reminder of who you were hinder who you are and will become. The apostle Paul said, "Nothing shall be able to separate us from the love of God, which is in Christ Jesus our Lord." (Romans 8:38-39 KJV) You have to remember there's no height, no depth, good, or bad that can separate you from God's love. Forgive yourself, so that you can be free. Whoever the Son, Jesus, has set free, is free—indeed.

When properly applied, forgiveness is beautiful and is a supreme representation of God's love for the Church. When we forgive the way God forgives, we show in the purest form that there's nothing that love can't cover.

If we walk in agape love, we won't go looking for an out. We won't "fall out of love" because love never falls. It never fails. We won't go looking for deal-breakers.

PART IV: PREPARE YOUR MARRIAGE FOR SUCCESS

10 NO DEAL BREAKERS

> *Love suffers long and is kind; love does not envy; love does not parade itself, is not puffed up; [5] does not behave rudely, does not seek its own, is not provoked, thinks no evil; [6] does not rejoice in iniquity, but rejoices in the truth; [7] bears all things, believes all things, hopes all things, endures all things. [8] Love never fails... (1 Corinthians 13:4-8a NKJV)*

The love in the 1 Corinthians passage is agape. It is unconditional, never-changing love. Love is a commitment that should stand and never fall. Love bears all things, believes all things, and hopes all things. Love never fails. If this is the love you embrace as your standard, then there should be no deal-breakers once you commit to a covenant—you have to enter the marriage understanding that it is "till death do us part."

Contract versus Covenant

One party can dissolve a contract when the other party does not hold up its end of the bargain. But covenants are everlasting. God covenanted with us, and regardless of what we do, God always holds up his end of the deal. Thus, it should be the same in a relationship between husband and wife. God designed marriage to emulate the relationship between Christ and the Church.

There can't be any deal-breakers once you enter a covenant. If you go into a marriage relationship with deal-breakers in your heart or mind, you're going into it under pretenses.

Jesus explained this to the Pharisees this way:

> And He answered and said to them, "Have you not read that He who made them at the beginning 'made them male and female,' [5] and said, 'For this reason a man shall leave his father and mother and be joined to his wife, and the two shall become one flesh'? [6] So then, they are no longer two but one flesh. Therefore what God has joined together, let not man separate." [7] They said to Him, "Why then did Moses command to give a certificate of divorce, and to put her away?" [8] He said to them, "Moses, because of the hardness of your hearts, permitted you to divorce your wives, but from the beginning, it was not so. [9] And I say to you, whoever divorces his wife, except for sexual immorality, and marries another, commits adultery; and whoever marries her who is divorced commits adultery." [10] His disciples said to Him, "If such is the case of the man with his wife, it is better not to marry." (Matthew 19:4-10 NKJV)

In his conversation with them, Jesus clarified that they divorced because of the hardness of their hearts. Divorces were happening all the time under the law (Deuteronomy 24:1-3). But Jesus reveals that the real reason that Moses had to give a writ of divorce was not adultery, but the hardness of their hearts.

Adultery was secondary. If you get a divorce, you cause infidelity. But the underlying problem that first leads to divorce is the hardness of heart. It is only because of the hardness of heart that divorce is necessary.

The heart can become hard if it's lost life through unforgiveness or bitterness, or lacks the nourishment of the Spirit. If we love the way God says we're supposed to love, operate in the Spirit (which is rivers of living water), and water our hearts with the word of God, our heart doesn't have to get to the point of hardness. But if we don't put the word of God into our hearts to wash it, and follow what it says regarding forgiveness, our hearts will get hard. It's then that we opt for divorce. It's not that God wanted the divorce, but it was the hardness of their hearts.

But Jesus shows us the way under the new covenant. He says:

> And I say to you, whoever divorces his wife, except for sexual immorality, and marries another, commits adultery; and whoever marries her who is divorced commits adultery." [10] His disciples said to Him, "If such is the case of the man with his wife, it is better not to marry." (Matthew 19:9-10 NKJV)

There can't be any deal-breakers; we have to enter the marriage union understanding that we will stick it out until death do us part. It has to be "'til death do us part" because God does not break his covenant with us. That's the love God wants us to have for one another.

We have to operate within the confines of the covenant.

Just because there are no deal-breakers, it does not mean we should act outside the confines of the covenant. While there may be grace because of the covenant, we want to heed the words of Paul, "Should we continue in sin that grace may abound. God forbid." So let's not take the grace for granted that's within a covenant. We understand that love hopes all things and endures all things, but we don't want to take that for granted or take advantage of that grace to sin. We don't want to take advantage of our covenant partner, either.

Covenants require sacrifice.

The concept of *no deal-breakers* also has to do with the mindset we need to enter marriage because covenants require sacrifice. Covenants are not convenient; they require sacrifice. God has done nothing for the sake of a covenant that was easy. Covenants always require the parties to give up something. God loved us, so he gave up and sacrificed his only Son so we could enter a covenant with him.

When God makes a covenant with Abraham, the first requirement was for him to leave his family. He had to leave what was familiar and made him comfortable. The same thing happens when you're in a marriage relationship. There are no deal-breakers. There may be times you have to leave your place of comfort. You may have to leave your family or move away from home.

Covenants can challenge you and reveal selfishness.

In covenant, when your spouse doesn't fulfill their responsibilities, it does not release you from yours. You don't have an out. You take responsibility for what you're supposed to do, even when your spouse doesn't fulfill their responsibilities.

Covenants always come with benefits and promises.

There is not one covenant in the Bible that did not come with the promise of being blessed. So when we make a covenant before God, it releases the anointing for us to prosper and grow. It releases an anointing for us to multiply. One of the first things God says to Adam and Eve is, "Be fruitful and multiply." God releases this blessing only in a marriage-covenant context. He does not release that blessing in a boyfriend and girlfriend context. The Bible says, "He who finds a wife finds a good thing, and obtains favor," not he who finds a girlfriend.

Thus, before you enter a marriage, understand that you are not entering a contract. You are entering a covenant that will require sacrifice. Have the mindset that there are no deal-breakers and that divorce is not an option. That mindset, coupled with appropriate boundaries, will help protect your marriage. In the next chapter, we discuss boundaries in detail.

11 BOUNDARIES

Boundaries are like a fortified wall around a city; for example, the City of Jericho. Building boundaries around your relationship is necessary so that, as with a wall, nothing can get in that needs to stay out or get out that needs to remain. That's the purpose of a wall. Its design keeps things in and keeps things out. The only way things should be able to get in is if you grant access.

Create effective boundaries to protect your relationship and keep it the way you want it—to keep it sustained. When you or your spouse give access to things that shouldn't be there, it depletes the resources that need to stay within your "city"; to remain within your relationship. Boundaries necessary for modern-day relationships can vary depending upon your history, depending on where you've been.

God never intended for divorce or children to be born outside of wedlock, but it's so prevalent now that it makes creating boundaries a difficult yet necessary thing to navigate. We have examples in the Bible that deal with difficult choices to create boundaries and protect a relationship. For example, blended families often confront coparenting issues.

Boundaries Regarding Blended Families That Have to Deal with Co-parents or Step-parents

One of the biggest challenges in a blended family is the reach that a coparent from a previous relationship has into the family household. That reach can bring negative impacts without boundaries.

For example, when there's a disagreement between your spouse and your coparent, who takes priority? What does the Bible say about it? And do we have a definitive example that we can use for guidance? Whenever feelings drive our decisions, we leave room for argument. But when the word of God informs our choices, all anyone can do is argue with God. Thankfully, there is a coparenting example in the Bible.

Abraham's relationships with Sarah and Hagar is the first baby mama drama in Scripture.

We understand that it was Sarah's suggestion to have Abraham sleep with Hagar, but that was not God's plan for Abraham's life. Similarly, we can have children outside of wedlock. God may allow it, but it was not a part of his perfect plan for our life. Because there is perfect and permissive will, God will make accommodations for our decisions—even those he did not want us to make. God doesn't take away choice and is omnipresent. He sees everything at all times. So it's not that God did it, but he knew what we would do and makes accommodations for our decisions. He even sometimes brings blessings out of them.

Sarah suggested that Abraham sleep with Hagar. Hagar got pregnant, and it created contention between Sarah and Hagar immediately. Why? The pregnancy made Hagar, the baby mama, feel she was superior to Sarah, the wife. Similarly, a baby mama or baby daddy who had children with you before you got married, may feel some superiority to your spouse who came afterward. And they think it gives them extended reach into your household because their child lives there.

Hagar had a superiority complex and disdain toward Sarah.

Sarah got upset and treated her harshly. So, there was a contention between Sarah and Hagar, and Abraham got stuck in the middle. What do you do when you're stuck in the middle of a contention between your spouse and your child's parent? Later, after Sarah had a son, she told Abraham to get rid of Hagar and the son he had with her because Hagar's son was making fun of her son.

What do you do, as a believer, when your spouse wants you to disconnect from your child and your baby's mama or baby's daddy? None of us would say—at least none of us in our right mind—would say, send them away. However, we find in the Scripture that this is precisely what Sarah said. She had no biblical precedent. She was the one who created the situation. She made this bed and didn't want to sleep in it. And when Abraham got stuck in this situation, God said to Abraham, "Listen to your wife."

> And Sarah saw the son of Hagar the Egyptian, which she had born unto Abraham, mocking. [10] Wherefore she said unto Abraham, Cast out this bondwoman and her son: for the son of this bondwoman shall not be heir with my son, even with Isaac. [11] And the thing was very grievous in Abraham's sight because of his son. [12] And God said unto Abraham, Let it not be grievous in thy sight because of the lad, and because of thy bondwoman; in all that Sarah hath said unto thee, hearken unto her voice; for in Isaac shall thy seed be called. [13] And also of the son of the bondwoman will I make a nation, because he is thy seed. [14] And Abraham rose up early in the morning, and took bread, and a bottle of water, and gave it unto Hagar, putting it on her shoulder, and the child, and sent her away: and she departed, and wandered in the wilderness of Beersheba. (Genesis 21:9-14 KJV)

Think about it. Ishmael had been there for fourteen years.

Ishmael had a relationship with his father. Ishmael didn't know what it was like to be without his dad. And God told Abraham, send your child away—not because God said it—but because his wife said it. God pinpointed the words of Sarah, the wife, to show that a covenant overrides everything.

A covenant made before God is God's priority. The covenant takes precedent. God said, send Hagar and Ishmael away. What did Abraham do? He gave Hagar one child support payment (some bread and water) and sent her away. That's all she got—one payment. The Scriptures never indicate that Abraham saw Ishmael again. Ishmael now has an absent father because the wife had an issue with the baby mama.

Abraham sent Hagar away because of a situation she didn't plan. Hagar got pregnant, and she didn't even ask for it. We would relate that to a modern-day, "I got pregnant on accident, I didn't even want this baby, and now suddenly, you're cutting me off because you got married to someone else?"

Abraham treated her like the mistress or the side chick. He sent her off with the baby and one child support payment, running into the wilderness. The wilderness often represents the unknown, the unfamiliar, or the desolate place. How difficult it must feel for anyone tasked with raising a child in that circumstance.

In her tears and hardship, God told Hagar that he would make a great nation out of Ishmael. So, even in the scenarios where God puts covenant first, he still takes care of all children involved. He is a father to the fatherless.

A father of the fatherless, a defender of widows, Is God in His holy habitation. (Psalm 68:5 NKJV)

You must establish boundaries for coparents, and there should also be boundaries for exes.

Boundaries Regarding Exes

Every relationship needs to have boundaries regarding exes. Identify the need (if any) for a continued relationship with an ex, especially if there are no children involved. If the relationship was romantic, the purpose of the relationship has ended. You now have a spouse, and that's the only romantic relationship you need.

Why is there still a purpose for that relationship? You are now in covenant and have become one with your spouse. Who can be closer to you? Whose opinion should be higher than your spouse? Why do you need this other perspective outside of Christ and your spouse? If your relationship is like that of Christ and the Church, what other perspective do you need outside of Christ to make decisions concerning your life?

You must realize there's no need for that relationship. Even if you try to keep them around in the category of "company," that extended relationship can be a threat to your fortified city. You and your spouse or potential spouse must discuss and agree on these boundaries.

The City of Jericho had the best fortification system known in biblical history. But eventually, after the Children of Israel circled the city long enough, the walls fell. Understand that these friendships that don't have defined boundaries, and that keep circling your relationship will eventually cause the walls in your relationship to fall. Jericho never thought their walls could fall, but they did.

Especially with past relationships, Paul made it clear to "flee youthful lusts." Flee also youthful lusts: but follow righteousness, faith, charity, peace, with them that call on the Lord out of a pure heart. (2 Timothy 2:22 KJV) And I don't know why we think we can entertain youthful lusts. If you slept with them, there's youthful lust there. If you were romantically involved enough to even think about sleeping with them, there was a youthful lust there. The Scripture says if you've thought about—slept with them in your heart—it's fornication.

> Ye have heard that it was said by them of old time, Thou shalt not commit adultery: [28] But I say unto you, That whosoever looketh on a woman to lust after her hath committed adultery with her already in his heart. (Matthew 5:27-28 KJV)

And that's a potential breach to your fortified city (your marriage relationship). Therefore, run from it and expel it out of your life. Run from it the way Joseph ran out of Potiphar's house. Flee youthful lusts. I don't care what you have to leave— you don't have to get your stuff back—get away from the relationships that threaten your marriage. Once again, protecting the marriage covenant should be your primary focus.

Boundaries With Family

Therefore shall a man leave his father and his mother, and shall cleave unto his wife: and they shall be one flesh. (Genesis 2:24 KJV)

Before you can cleave to a spouse effectively, you must leave your family. That doesn't mean no contact at all, but you have to leave and disconnect emotionally. Your family can't be the first place you run to when things get hard in life because now you are doing life with your spouse. And in the light of negative family influences, make sure you understand that the family you're trying to build now may have to differ drastically from the one in which you grew up.

When God called Abram to leave Terah, his family served idol gods. God called Abram to leave his family, disconnect from idol gods, and serve the one true God. There may be some things we have glorified in the family upbringing that we should now tear down. Sometimes, we allow the voice of our parents to become the idol in our marriage. Sometimes a parent's opinion has too much influence on a marriage. Sometimes a sister's opinion has too much impact on a marriage.

Sometimes, family traditions have too much impact on marriage because the spouses' job now is to build new traditions together. But if we don't have effective boundaries and we don't discuss the need for them, family opinions and traditions can tear down the covenant that a husband and wife have built.

We have to know how to create boundaries, disconnect, and identify what's beneficial and what's not. And you do that through communication and choice. Choices could include where to spend holidays, who to invite to family dinners, who's coming over, and how frequently. Make those choices and establish them as boundaries.

The marriage will always be the priority over everything, so you have to establish boundaries with family members.

Boundaries Regarding Children

It is best to establish proper boundaries with children before entering a marriage, especially if there are children from previous relationships, or if children were present in the home before getting married. Lack of boundaries with children can create frustrations. To ensure the marriage is healthy, make sure that even the children don't become the priority over the marriage.

Rebekah favored her son, Jacob, over his brother, Esau. She loved Jacob so much that she helped him deceive her husband because there weren't effective boundaries with her child. She got too involved with one son, and broke an ordinance that God established for the family.

Children need boundaries, or they will not respect the parents appropriately. Would Jacob had been more respectful of his father if he had not seen his mother undermine him? If you do not establish boundaries between parents and children early, the children can undermine the authority in the house.

If a parent speaks to a child as an equal (especially in the presence of a spouse), it can cause problems. For example, if a male child is the only male in the house, the mother can treat him as the male counterpart of that house. Especially in African-American culture, you may hear people tell him, "You're the man of the house now." But that creates a lack of boundaries because he sees himself as an equal. When a man shows up as a new spouse, there is a contention between the spouse and the male child.

Another example is letting kids sleep in bed with a single parent. Think of the difficulty that creates for a new spouse coming into their life. The children will no longer sleep in the bed, and that can create contention because the children may feel like the new spouse is taking their parent away from them.

Children have to be children at all times. In discipline, they have to be children. In opinion, they have to be children. Your marriage must be the priority at all times. If a spouse feels that the children are getting more from their spouse than they are, it can create deficiencies. You want your spouse to feel that you reciprocate their love at all times.

12 RECIPROCATION

When I met Rey, my current wife, I told her I struggled with feeling like I was too affectionate. Even though it was one of my love languages, I never felt like I received equal reciprocation in that area from my previous spouses. It always left me frustrated. I felt like I had to water down who I was as a person to ensure I was not overbearing or feel like I was doing too much. I explained that, in past relationships, they made me feel like an addict, and I was going to hell because I desired sexual intimacy so often. I never thought three or four times a week was too often for someone in their early thirties, but maybe it was. Her response was, "I think we'll be just fine."

When we finally decided we would move ahead with a romantic relationship, I opened the car door for her the first time and naturally grabbed her hand to help her out of the car. She grabbed it back. When we left the restaurant, she reached out for my hand, and I grabbed it back.

The next time I saw her, I grabbed the door and opened it so she could get out of the car. She reached for my hand; I grabbed it back. That has continued throughout our relationship. There's never a time that we don't hold hands when we get out of the car—a sign of affection that's important to me.

If I make her plate, she'll make my plate next. If I tell her I love her when I get off the phone, she tells me she loves me the next time we get on the phone. We have a constant give and take, which keeps our "relational account balance" full.

Relationships are like a bank account. In an account, there are deposits and withdrawals. When there are too many withdrawals and not enough deposits, there are fees—insufficiencies. Sometimes, in a relationship, one party puts too much demand on the other party to make all the deposits and maintain the weight of the relationship.

For a relationship to be healthy, there needs to be equal deposits and withdrawals from each spouse. That is reciprocation. Reciprocation is the habit of regular deposits and withdrawals and giving and taking that makes a relationship solid. There's a security in knowing that what you give, and as much as you give, you'll get back from your spouse. It keeps you secure, safe, and consistent.

Often, spouses underestimate the importance of reciprocation. Regardless of the number of relationships I've been in, I'm grateful that I'm finally in one that has consistent reciprocation. I never feel like I'm too much, and I never feel like I'm not getting enough.

For a relationship to thrive, there should be a habit of reciprocation. You can't have one party giving and one party taking all the time. Both parties have to give and take equally. When reciprocation is not present, the account can end up being overdrawn. When an account remains overdrawn too long, it can lead to an account closure.

What does reciprocation look like in marriage?

Reciprocation applies in many areas of the relationship. With finances, reciprocation is necessary. One party cannot feel like they're financially contributing more than the other party all the time without feeling like they are getting a return on their investment.

Men specifically, rarely do anything, whether something monetary or not, without expecting a return on their investment. I believe that anytime a man gives a woman money or offers to do something for a woman, there is a latent expectation of something in return. Remember, Adam was the first farmer. He knew that sowing a seed would and *should* yield a harvest.

So in a marriage, there is a commitment to provide and an expectation of a response to that provision. That equates to reciprocation. If the husband provides all the money, he'll expect his wife to maintain the home. Conversely, if the wife provides, it would be appropriate for her to expect the husband to manage the home. If marriage is a team approach, you fill in the gaps for each other to keep the home functioning. Lack of reciprocation removes incentive and motivation and creates the risk of one party ceasing its efforts to maintain the relationship.

Reciprocation is effective when you understand each other's needs. Reciprocation means different things to different people. So, understanding the needs of your mate is monumental.

For example, a man may need three things: a clean house, cooked dinner, and sexual intimacy. He may need nothing else but those three things. A wife can do fifteen things, but if she does not meet one of those three things, he will feel she is not reciprocating his effort.

Similarly, a husband can be a good provider and protector. He can meet all the financial needs of the family. However, if the needs of the wife are words of affirmation, quality time, or gifts, none of the other things he does will equate to reciprocation for her.

Meeting your spouse's needs should be at the top of your priority list. Without needs being met, spouses can go into "survival mode" and do whatever is necessary to get them met. God promises to meet our needs. He sacrificed his only begotten son to meet our need for salvation; we should emulate his sacrifice and do the same for our spouse.

Throughout this book, I have shared my personal experiences with transparency. I hope you gained insight to confront issues I didn't have wisdom for at the time. For me, the lessons in this book are invaluable and life-changing. I'm happy to say that I am finally enjoying a loving marriage relationship, and I pray you will too.

ABOUT THE AUTHOR

Earnest Fitzhugh, II, has been preaching since his teens and has been in pastoral ministry since 2009. His preaching ministry started at 17 years old and he was licensed at age 19. A year later, he was ordained as an elder by the late Bishop LeRoy Robert Anderson. He served as an associate elder of Higher Ground Church of God in Christ in Phoenix, AZ, where his father is pastor, until the founding and launch of New Covenant Church of God in Christ in September of 2009. Despite significant challenges, God has blessed Pastor Fitzhugh to apply clarity to the assignment of the church, memorialized when name was changed to Redemption Life Center. Redemption has become a hub of transition and growth for all people, regardless of their past difficulties, current disposition or cultural background.

Pastor Fitzhugh is a native of Phoenix, Arizona. His college course of study and largest portion of employment history is in the area of Law. He's built and owned multiple successful businesses and has a true heart for entrepreneurship. Pastor Fitzhugh has a God given grace for ministry development and marketing as it relates to this generation of believer. An effective communicator and teacher of God's Word, Pastor Fitzhugh is widely known for his practical and dynamic teaching style which helps people apply the timeless truths of Scripture to their everyday lives. Pastor Fitzhugh has traveled various places teaching his Kairos Leadership Program. A program designed to assist churches/leadership in assess its current efficacy as it relates to conversion and retention of new believers.

He and his wife, "Rey," proudly parent four children and continue to aspire to do God's work and be an example for those around them. Pastor Fitzhugh often says, "Where I am today, makes everything I went through, worth it. All things really do work together for the good."

For more information about the author, visit www.realationshipsbook.com.

www.ingramcontent.com/pod-product-compliance
Lightning Source LLC
LaVergne TN
LVHW051507070426
835507LV00022B/2972